FORM AND COLOUR

SANDRO BOTTICELLI / THE NATIVITY

SANDRO BOTTICELLI
THE NATIVITY

WITH AN INTRODUCTION BY
LIONELLO VENTURI PH. D.
PROFESSOR AT THE UNIVERSITY OF ROME

LONGMANS, GREEN AND CO
LONDON · NEW YORK · TORONTO

ALESSANDRO FILIPEPI called BOTTICELLI

The composition of this picture has a spiritual rather than a visual unity. The single episodes, however, are built up towards the centre where the Virgin is adoring the Child, with Saint Joseph, the ox and the ass under the thatched roof of a hut at the rocky entrance to a cave. The fact that these figures are somewhat larger than the others, proves that in the mind of the artist they are the most important; the other images are only a commentary on the main subject. Botticelli knew perfectly well the rules of perspective, but in this picture he did not follow them, because his aim was not to represent space but to present images of his state of mind. Hence, he painted in the middle ground figures larger than those in the foreground. This is not disproportion, but a moral proportion substituted for visual.

The form of the figures has the same character as the composition. Botticelli was a master of plastic form, owing to his command of the nuances of chiaroscuro and thus he knew how to obtain a realistic representation of the human form. But he felt that by putting an accent on line he could emphasize the expression of the soul. The anxiety of the Virgin's adoration and the affectionate longing of the Child towards His Mother are expressed by the curved line which unites the group. The intense concentration of Saint Joseph's worship is expressed, not by his face, which is covered, but by the winding line of his body. Line is indeed for Botticelli the way to reach intensity of expression, either tender and full of piety in the group of the Virgin and Child, or dramatic in the image of Saint Joseph.

Fifteenth-century painters have often combined the subject matter of the *Nativity* with that of the *Adoration of the Shepherds*. Botticelli has isolated the scene of the Nativity, but to the right, outside the hut, he has depicted two shepherds brought by an angel to adore the new-born Christ. At the left, symmetrically, he has painted three other men, crowned like the shepherds with olive leaves, brought also by another angel to bow to Christ. These are not so much individuals as they are representative images of mankind.

Again in the foreground, three men, also olive-crowned, are embracing angels. From left to right there is an increasing intensity of feeling. The first group expresses only tenderness, but the second one shows a sense of danger escaped, and the third an outburst of surprise at a salvation despaired of. At the corners two devils fleeing under the rocks show what the danger had been and reveal the meaning of the scene to be a redemption from hell.

These events are imagined in an earthly setting, among rocks and meadows, bounded by a curtain of dark trees in the background. Botticelli likes pure colours, red, blue, green, yellow, pink, white and applies them against a dark background, in order to harmonize them with the chiaroscuro and throw them into relief. But the clear colours of the rocks give a certain complexity to the background, and thus lighten the effect of relief.

The upper part of the picture has a different vision and a different meaning. The thatched roof of the hut shows some touches of gold. Beyond them, we enter a world which belongs not to earth, but to Heaven. Three angels on the roof sing God's praises. Above, twelve other angels dance among olive branches, against a clear blue sky, and in the golden light of Paradise.

Beyond the earth, in the open space, Botticelli dreams in brilliant colours, either dark on light, or the reverse, and here the painting is beyond mere scenic representation. His undulating lines gain emphasis from the slender bodies of the angels and thus create rhythms which have a value of their own. The plastic quality necessary to the representation of reality is almost forgotten.

This dreamlike *motif* allows the artist to express his state of mind, without any limit or obstacle, in a diffused way, with ease and incomparable charm. His angels are full of grace and tenderness, but they are not happy; a vague, strange melancholy envelops them; they are not children, they remember long-past sorrows. They express no anxiety as do the figures in the foreground; they are near the light of God, and their recollections are softened by their heavenly ritual.

By interpreting the lines and the colours, we may perhaps understand the mystic symbolism of the picture. Men who have just escaped from the temptations of the devil find peace in the embraces of the angels. A further step is their approach to the new-born Child, the Nativity being not only an historical event, but also that everyday event by which a man finds God in himself. Then he can see beyond this earth, he can dream of the light of Paradise, of the singing angels, of the peace of God in Christ. Thus the *motif* of Botticelli's *Nativity* is a meditation on the Christian mystery, on the way of salvation.

Historical data can clarify, and at the same time widen, the meaning of the picture. At the top of it a Greek inscription has been deciphered and translated by Herbert Horne:

'I, Sandro, painted this picture, at the end of the year 1500 (March 24th, 1501, of the Roman Calendar) during the troubles of Italy, in the half year after the first year of the three and a half years, of the loosing of the devil, in accordance with the fulfilment of the eleventh chapter of Saint John, in the second woe of the Apocalypse; then he shall be chained according to the twelfth chapter, and we shall see him trodden down as in this picture.'

To understand this inscription, it is well to know something of the troubles of Italy and particularly of Florence during the years before the beginning of 1501, when the *Nativity* was painted.

In 1492, Lorenzo de'Medici died. He had been the master of Florence for more than twenty years, and had promoted and now almost personified the most brilliant period of Florentine civilization, one of the most glorious epochs of creative art, the most active moment of the Italian Renaissance. His politics, though unstable, had maintained an uneasy equilibrium among the rulers of Italy, and consequently a state of peace. But immediately after his death, a long series of invasions, wars and disorders shook Italian life and ruined Florentine power.

A Dominican friar, Girolamo Savonarola, who began to preach in Florence in 1489, condemned the decay of morals, tried to reform the Church, and sought to make the Pope, Alexander Borgia, responsible for all the misery of the times. He prophesied the coming disasters and his prophecy seemed to be fulfilled when Charles VIII, King of France, invaded Italy in 1494. Savonarola then entered politics, but he was unable to keep the evils of war, famine and plague from the city and, after losing his popularity, was condemned to death and burnt in the public square of Florence in 1498.

Simone Filipepi, a brother of Botticelli, and faithful follower of Savonarola, refers in his chronicle to a discussion on November 2, 1499, between Doffo Spini, one of those who had condemned Savonarola, and Sandro Botticelli in the latter's workshop:

'And in effect, upon Sandro questioning him... that he should tell him the plain truth as to what faults they found in Fra Girolamo, by which he deserved to die so infamous a death: whereat Doffo then replied to him: "Sandro, have I to tell you the truth? Not only did we never find in him mortal sin: but, moreover, neither was venial sin found in him." Then Sandro said to him: "Wherefore did you cause him to die in so infamous a fashion?" He replied: "Not I, but Benozzo Federighi was the cause of it. And if this prophet and his companions had not been put

to death and had they been sent back to San Marco, the people would have put us to sack, and we should all have been cut to pieces. The matter had so far gone forward, that thus we determined for our safety, that they should die".'*

All this illuminates Botticelli's reaction to the death of Savonarola. Even one of the judges of the friar admitted that he was a martyr. Botticelli had no doubt of it. His sincere Christian feeling, the reality of the disasters prophesied, the part taken by his brother, a sincere follower of the friar, all this proves that Botticelli resented the martyrdom of Savonarola, as a new crucifixion of the Lord.

The prophecy of Savonarola and that of Saint John were connected in the mind of Botticelli, and recalling Saint John's period of three and a half years allotted for the triumph of the devil on earth, he interpreted the actual events around him. No doubt, the devil had been loosed after the death of Savonarola, which took place only a few months before the one and a half years indicated by the inscription.

But who was the devil?

Cesare Borgia, the Duke Valentino, the son of the pope, was in 1500 at the height of his power. After murdering his own brother, the Duke of Gandia, and marrying a kinswoman of the King of France, he had conquered the Romagna, committed all sorts of crimes, and had entered Tuscany by taking Piombino. In the following year he did great damage in the territory of Florence. The Florentines were deeply apprehensive, expecting that Florence would share the same fate as the towns in the Romagna. This was their state of mind when Botticelli painted his *Nativity*.

Thus the devil loosed on earth was Cesare Borgia, and Botticelli was looking forward to two more years of disaster, and then to the new chaining of the devil, to the new birth of Christ, and to the new peace on earth, according to the Revelation of Saint John. He painted not what he saw, but what he hoped. From the pit of disaster, he was able to see the angels dancing in Paradise.

Botticelli was born in Florence 1444 or 1445, son of a poor artisan. About 1459 he entered the workshop of Fra Filippo Lippi, who had been, but was no longer, of the advance guard in painting. However, Botticelli was soon able to master perspective and anatomy, the two sciences which had opened the way to an objective representation of the outside world. Furthermore, under the influence of Antonio Pollaiuolo, Botticelli understood the importance of the contour line in order to give movement to the body, through which can be represented movement of the soul. But, unlike Pollaiuolo's, Botticelli's line was seldom used for dramatic expression: he preferred to contemplate undulating lines and enjoy their rhythms leading to that kind of beauty which is grace.

Fra Filippo Lippi was a devout man, but his passionate sensuousness compelled him to look at this world only, without any transcendent inspiration. Antonio Pollaiuolo belonged to the new type of the Florentine Renaissance man, the conqueror of the outside world, whose moral value consisted in his strong vitality, in his energy, in his grandeur. Sandro Botticelli was a religious Christian soul, more so than any of the prominent artists of his time in Florence; thus he assimilated and mastered the new artistic science of the Renaissance, without forgetting the contemplation of the unseen, the presence of the outer world inside his heart. This is the reason why, beyond his masterful drawing, we always feel his need to dream, to sigh and to love.

His contemporaries appreciated in him above all his 'virile air, great judgment and perfect

* The translation is by Herbert Horne.

10

sense of proportion.' In the sixteenth century Vasari saw in Botticelli's *Saint Augustine* a profound 'cogitation and most acute subtlety, generally found in persons of sense who are continually occupied with the investigation of very elevated and difficult things.'

In later times, Botticelli was forgotten, and was rediscovered by English writers between 1867 and 1871, by Dante Gabriel Rossetti, A. C. Swinburne, Walter Pater and John Ruskin. They discovered in Botticelli the forerunner of the modern romanticists and decadents. Walter Pater emphasized the 'peculiar sentiment with which he infuses his profane and sacred persons, comely, and in a certain sense like angels, but with a sense of displacement or loss about them — the wistfulness of exiles, conscious of a passion and energy greater than any known issue of them explains, which runs through all his varied work with a sense of ineffable melancholy.'

Without any doubt, both the Italians of the Renaissance and the English of the nineteenth century were right, but each of them saw only one aspect of the art of Botticelli. His mastery of the most perfect knowledge his time could offer him did not satisfy his yearning towards the transcendental faith of Christianity. He did not find his poetry within the reality he saw, but continually transcended reality to reach the world of his dreams.

From 1470, it seems that Lorenzo de'Medici was his patron, and he worked for him and for other members of the Medici family. Botticelli was a great artist, but he conceived himself as an artisan who must do as he is ordered. Thus, he was ready to put the portraits of the Medici family into an *Adoration of the Magi*: these portraits are beautiful, but have nothing to do with the religious theme. Furthermore, to decorate the rooms of the Medici, he painted mythological scenes, of which the *Spring* and the *Birth of Venus* are the most famous. But the intimate feeling of the artist reveals itself, in spite of everything. Botticelli's Venus betrays a consciousness of sin: he paints Venus but thinks of Magdalen.

The commissions of the Medici gave him great renown, both in and beyond Florence. However, while connoisseurs appreciated his 'virile air' and his 'perfect sense of proportion', simpler people were attracted by his Madonnas. No painter of his time had so many demands for Madonnas, and his pupils repeated more and more his *motifs*. Simple people perhaps saw in them only devout images, but the art of Botticelli goes far beyond devotion. His Madonnas are not childhood dreams like those of Fra Angelico; they are conscious of worldly sins; their forms are too powerfully human to deprive them of the sense of reality. They are suspended between heaven and earth, and participate in that interpenetration of the spiritual and the material which is grace.

This uncertainty of Botticelli hovering between the two orders of moral feeling and creative imagination, is responsible for his appeal to us, for his actuality, as the English writers saw. For the people of the fifteenth century this uncertainty meant that the painter was the representative in art of that crisis of conscience which led to Savonarola and the Reformation. The Renaissance had started with a new conception of Christian religion, emphasizing faith in man, as a microcosm where the universe was mirrored. But the decay of morals brought so many troubles and so much arbitrary anarchy, that a crisis developed towards the end of the fifteenth century. Savonarola was one of the many voices raised to give mankind a consciousness of its decay, the strongest voice before Luther. Their only suggestion to cure that decay was to return to the Middle Ages, when faith in Christ was much more alive. Of course, a return was impossible. Thus arose the uncertainty between the dream of a purer life and the sense of the actual reality. Botticelli's art was the artistic form of that uncertainty.

It often happens that artists anticipate the spiritual trends of mankind. Thus before 1490,

Botticelli had expressed his uncertainty by indulging in his masterly skill and by dreaming of idyllic grace. But towards 1490 his line becomes sharp, there is a departure from the 'perfect sense of proportion', and we are conscious of an agitation which is not without grandeur in its intense inwardness, an intensity of colouring which seeks to make itself independent of chiaroscuro, finally a dramatic expression of anxiety, of anguish, of new aspirations.

At about the time of the *Nativity* he painted the *Crucifixion* (now in the Fogg Museum, Cambridge, Mass.). On the right of the Cross, an angel is holding a rod in his right hand, and in his left an animal which seems to be a fox, recalling the Song of Solomon against the foxes which ruin the vineyards. From the sky, where God the Father is seated, various shields adorned with a cross descend on clouds where a number of devils send fire on to the earth. The fire approaches the walls of Florence, a view of which forms the background. This is the punishment for its sins predicted for Florence by Savonarola. But the tall figure of Magdalen embracing the foot of the cross is calling for mercy. Perhaps the anatomical drawing is not correct, but Botticelli needs to be free from any rule in order to give tremendous strength to the expression. The Magdalen, in her desperate hope, is the intimate voice of the artist, the spiritual centre of the whole picture.

In later years, in the *Episodes from the Life of Saint Zenobius* (Dresden Gallery; National Gallery, London; Metropolitan Museum, New York) his colouring assumes a new intensity, based on contrasts of single tints. They do not produce an effect of light and shade, they are outcries of despair. So are the sharp lines, which lose their beloved rhythm, and become the accents of the painter's anguish. So are the simplified planes, with a chiaroscuro reduced to the minimum.

Botticelli died in 1510 in seclusion and silence. The devil had not been chained. The world around him could no longer understand him. He was one of the few who remembered the years of peace both in public life and in the intimate conscience.

Ten years before, when he painted the *Nativity* he had expressed his hope in the embrace of men and angels, in the rebirth of Christ, in the contemplation of angels dancing in the light of Paradise. From his hope his brush had received the strength to create again grace and tenderness, to overcome anguish, to reach that serenity which is proper to the highest art. He had not painted it as an altar-piece or for public view, he had even written in Greek the explanatory inscription in order to avoid eventual persecution. He painted it for himself, in order to express his innermost feeling, his most secret hope. So he reached an intimacy, a sincerity, a concentration, which are as rare in his work as in the works of all artists and all epochs.

Longmans, Green and Co Ltd
6 & 7 Clifford Street London W 1
Also at Melbourne and Cape Town
Longmans, Green and Co Inc
55 Fifth Avenue New York 3
Longmans, Green and Co
215 Victoria Street Toronto 1
Orient Longmans Ltd
Bombay Calcutta Madras

First published 1949

Plates made by Algemeene Cliché Industrie, Amsterdam
and printed by De Jong & Co, Hilversum
Text set in 16 points Foundry *Garamond*
Typography H. van Krimpen

Printed in the Netherlands